sundance

LITTLE GREEN
R E A D E R S

Garbage
Detectives

Focus: Recycling

Meredith Costain

Josh and I are garbage detectives.

We look for clues in
the garbage at our school.
Maybe some of it can
be recycled.

Monday 9:00 a.m.

We checked the wastepaper baskets. They were full of paper.

We made some suggestions.

- Write on both sides of the paper.
- Staple used paper together to make notepads.
- Recycle used paper.

Monday 10:00 a.m.

We found a full basket
of paper near the
copy machine.

We made some suggestions.

- Ask teachers to use both sides of the paper when they copy things.
- Ask teachers to write more things on the blackboard.

Monday 12:00 p.m.
We checked the school trash cans. We found many glass bottles and aluminum cans inside.

We made some suggestions.

- Recycle used cans and bottles.
- Ask kids to use plastic drink bottles that can be used again.

Monday 1:00 p.m.

We found lunch bags and candy wrappers in the trash cans. The bags and wrappers were made from paper and plastic. We found apple cores, orange peels, and banana skins, too.

We made some suggestions.

- Ask kids to use lunch boxes that can be used again.
- Start a worm farm. Use earthworms to recycle food scraps.

Monday 2:00 p.m.

We checked the schoolyard. We found lots of leaves and grass clippings.

We made some suggestions.

- Start a compost heap in the garden. Put the leaves and grass clippings on the compost heap. Use the compost next year to grow flowers.

We made a compost heap.
When the compost is ready,
we can add it to the soil
in the school garden. It will
help to make the soil rich.

Does your school have a lot of garbage? You could try our suggestions, too.

Glossary

compost	a mixture of rotting and moldy food that is added to soil
core	middle
grass clippings	pieces of grass that have been cut
recycle	to use again
scraps	small pieces
suggestions	ideas
wrappers	covers